Dynamic Faith Journal

Jerry Falwell

with

Rod Dempsey

World Publishing
Since 1928

Published by World Publishing, Inc., Nashville, TN 37214
www.worldpublishing.com

Printed in the United States of America
1 2 3 4 5 — 09 08 07 06 05

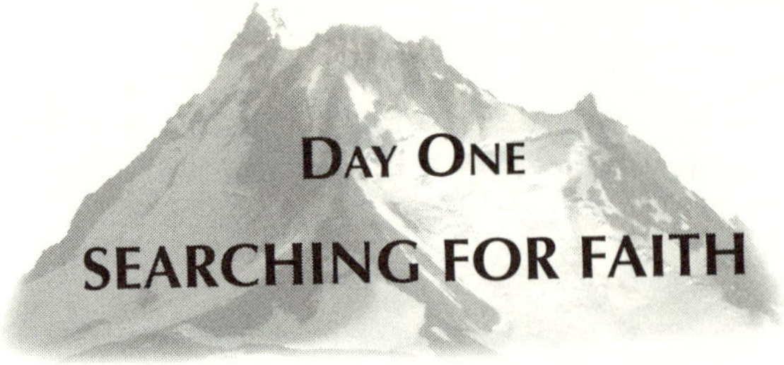

Day One

Searching for Faith

Scripture Reading: Mark 9:14–29

Verse: "If you can believe, all things are possible to him who believes." (Mark 9:23)

Meditation:

Do you remember the first time you stepped out in faith and believed God? Perhaps it was when you trusted Christ for your salvation. Maybe it was a verse that you read in God's Word, and by faith you acted in obedience. It could have been the first time you went to God in prayer and asked for something only God could have provided. Dr. Falwell's first great faith experience came when he was a freshman in Bible college and he failed as a Sunday school teacher of 11-year-old boys. That failure pushed Jerry to the prayer closet, which led him to take action and recruit for his Sunday school class all the 11-year-old boys he could find. As a result, at the end of a year his class had grown from 1 to 56.

No matter what pushes you to trust God, the Christian life is lived by faith. Consider what Romans 1:17 says: "The just shall live by faith." Every step of obedience you take in the Christian life is a step of faith. On this first day of your journey toward a more dynamic faith, Dr. Falwell asks you to write down one thing God is saying to you right now. It may develop as you go through this 31-day journey, but right now, what is one thing you believe God wants you to do?

Your Faith Journal Entry

Day Two

THE THINGS GOD USES

Scripture Reading: 1 Timothy 3:15–17; 2 Timothy 1:5–6

Verse: "But you [Timothy] must continue in the . . . Scriptures, which are able to make you wise for salvation through faith which is in Christ Jesus." (2 Timothy 3:14–15)

Meditation:

What was your life like B.C., "Before Christ"? Were you antagonistic around Christians or just apathetic? Maybe you didn't have any feelings or emotions toward Christ and Christians. Perhaps your view toward Christians was something like, "If they don't bother me, I won't bother them." Often, when we take the time to reflect, as Dr. Falwell does in this day's reading, we come to discover we have had several influences and situations whereby we encountered the good news of Jesus Christ. In Jerry's case, his mother tuning the radio to the "Old Fashioned Revival Hour" and the witness of a godly young man at "Boys State" planted lasting seeds.

What about you? What were some influences that encouraged you to make a commitment to Christ? As you think about it, you may conclude that you really don't have a personal relationship with Christ yet. If that is the case, the Scripture is very clear: "Today is the day of salvation . . . now is the appointed time" (see 2 Cor. 6:2). Your action point for today is simple: Open your heart to Jesus and ask Him to forgive your sins and to come into your life and take control. If you've already done that, jot down some important influences and how they helped you come to know Christ in a personal way.

Your Faith Journal Entry

Day Three

OVERCOMING ROADBLOCKS TO GOD

Scripture Reading: Mark 7:24–37

Verse: "For whoever calls on the name of the LORD shall be saved." (Romans 10:13)

Meditation:

In this day's reading Dr. Falwell recounts the story of how his dad, an avowed agnostic, came to know Christ in a personal way. Many obstacles stood in the way of this hardened businessman coming to Christ, but through the persistent prayers of his wife and his daughter, he came to Christ on his deathbed.

We all have obstacles in our lives when it comes to knowing and following Christ. You may have past hurts and present habits that hinder you. You may have a nagging hang-up that feels impossible to overcome. Or you may be a believer, but you have someone in your family who doesn't know Christ and you are concerned for that person. Today, you and I must realize that the only way to God is through His Son, Jesus Christ. Jesus Himself said in John 14:6, "I am the way, the truth, and the life. No one comes to the Father except through Me."

Your assignment for today is twofold. First, make a list of two or three things that have kept you from God in the past. How were these obstacles overcome? What did you do? What did others do? Second, write down names of two or three people about whom you are concerned. Begin praying that God would open their eyes so that they can see their need for Christ.

Your Faith Journal Entry

Day Four

YOU HAVE TO MAKE A CHOICE

Scripture Reading: Luke 18:18–30

Verse: "But as many as received Him, to them He gave the right to become children of God, to those who believe in His name." (John 1:12)

Meditation:

The dictionary defines *believe* in this manner: "to accept as true or real and to have faith, confidence and trust." What are some things you believe in? Make a short list in your journal, things like, "I believe in God" or "I believe in freedom" or "I believe the chair in my family room can hold me up when I sit down." Every day we exercise confidence and trust in the things in and around our households. For example, whenever we are driving our automobiles and we apply the brakes, we are exercising faith that those brakes are going to do their job and stop the car.

Believing in Christ requires that you voluntarily place your faith in the fact that when He died on the cross, He was dying in your place and paying for your sins. The Bible tells us in John 3:16: "For God so loved the world that He gave His only begotten Son, that whoever believes in Him should not perish but have everlasting life." The gospel message is that simple, but it requires that you believe. Dr. Falwell placed faith in Jesus Christ on January 20, 1952. In your journal today, write how you came to know Christ and how God has changed your life since that time.

Your Faith Journal Entry

Day Five

DEVELOPING A DREAM

Scripture Reading: Habakkuk 2

Verse: "Then the Lord answered and said to me, 'Write down the vision I give to you so those on the path of life can read and understand it. The vision may be for the future, but eventually you will see the completion of the vision.'" (Habakkuk 2:2–3, Falwell's translation)

Meditation:

Every so often we remember our dreams when we wake up. Sometimes those dreams are very pleasing to us, sometimes not. All of us dream at night, but not many of us have dreams while we are awake, and even fewer of us have spiritual dreams. In today's reading, Dr. Falwell shares with us that "every person was put here on this earth for a reason. The reason that God put you here is really spelled out in His dream for your life." What is a dream God is putting in your heart and on your mind? In Jerry's case, it was to build a church and a university on 4,000 acres of Liberty Mountain.

Your dream may not be that large, but if God wants you to do it, it is no less significant. In your journal, write your answer to this question: "If you could do anything for God's kingdom and glory, what would you really like to do?" Your answer to that question will go a long way to help you realize God's dream for your life. God saved you so you can help others. How can you take your gifts, your talents, and your abilities and be a blessing to others? As you write the answers to these questions, it is quite possible you will begin to dream during your waking hours.

Your Faith Journal Entry

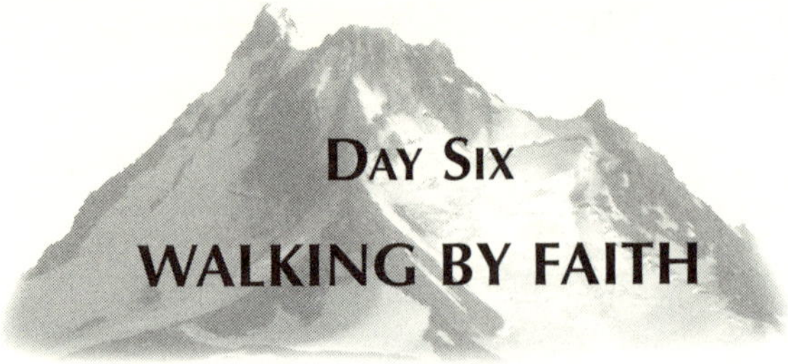

Day Six

WALKING BY FAITH

Scripture Reading: Joshua 14:6–15

Verse: "For we walk by faith, not by sight." (2 Corinthians 5:7)

Meditation:

People enjoy taking a walk for many reasons. It is good exercise. It's a good way to clear your head and think about things from a different perspective. If you go with a friend, it is a good way to catch up on the day's or week's events.

Our walk with God is similar, because today's verse reminds us that walking with God is a faith proposition. Walking by faith simply means we don't have it all planned out exactly. Sometimes we must wait to see what God wants to do through us and how He wants to do it. In today's reading, Dr. Falwell shares with us the story of how God provided a $100 million building for the grand total of a one-dollar lease payment. This is a modern-day miracle, and it shows that God is still in the miracle business.

You may not need a miracle, but walking with God involves walking by faith. It means we may not know exactly what God is going to do, but we are convinced He is going to do something amazing—something that only He can get the credit for. In today's assignment, Dr. Falwell wants you to ask yourself again, "What is the main thing God wants me to do?" As you write that out, also ask yourself this: "What activities will help me accomplish that purpose?"

Your Faith Journal Entry

Day Seven

GETTING WITH GOD

Scripture Reading: Psalm 84:1–12

Verse: "Call to Me and I will answer you, and show you great and mighty things, which you do not know." (Jeremiah 33:3)

Meditation:

God is a real person, and He desires that we spend time every day reading His words, talking and listening to Him. Psalm 27:8 puts it this way: "When You said, 'Seek My face,' my heart said to You, 'Your face, O LORD, I will seek.'" This is called "getting with God." When we get together with God on a regular basis, He begins to change us from the inside out. In today's reading, Dr. Falwell makes this statement, "If there's any secret to stronger faith, it's developing a stronger prayer life. That's the key to reaching your dreams and overcoming obstacles in your life."

In your journal today, write down some things you are praying for right now. You may be praying for your children, your parents, your work, your church, your ministry . . . and so forth. There are lots of things to pray for, but make a list and put a date beside each request. Watch how many of those requests the Lord takes care of in a short amount of time. Remember, though, God doesn't want you to seek just His hand; He wants you to seek His face.

Your Faith Journal Entry

Day Eight

GROWING OUR FAITH

Scripture Reading: Luke 9:23, 26, 57–62

Verse: "Then He said to them all, 'If anyone desires to come after Me, let him deny himself, and take up his cross daily, and follow Me.'" (Luke 9:23)

Meditation:

Have you ever noticed a newborn baby when he or she gets hungry? The only thing that can satisfy that hunger is pure milk! The baby will "pitch a fit" if he or she doesn't receive milk in a hurry. The Bible tells us in 1 Peter 2:2 that we should be "like newborn babes, longing for the pure milk of the Word, that by it you may grow in respect to salvation." When it comes to growing, we should imitate babies and their desire for milk. When we take in the milk of the Word, it will enable us to grow spiritually.

In today's reading, Dr. Falwell shares with us that we must learn to "love the Word of God and master its contents." One way to accomplish this goal is to read the Bible on a daily basis and to regularly attempt to memorize Scripture verses and passages. In your journal today, jot down your favorite ways to get into the Scriptures, and also note some creative ways you could begin memorizing the Word of God. Remember, growing your faith means you must come to the place where not only do you desire the "pure milk of the Word," but you are consuming the Word on a daily basis.

Your Faith Journal Entry

Day Nine

PUTTING YOUR LIFE PLAN TO WORK

Scripture Reading: Acts 1:1–11

Verse: "But you shall receive power when the Holy Spirit has come upon you; and you shall be witnesses to Me in Jerusalem, and in all Judea and Samaria, and to the end of the earth." (Acts 1:8)

Meditation:

Every person should ask himself or herself three important questions. The first is "Who am I?" The second is "Why am I here?" And the third is "Where am I going?" The way you answer these questions will help you discover your life purpose. In answer to the first question, take into consideration the things you enjoy doing. If you know a bit about your personality or temperament, write a little about these things. As you answer the second question, review things you enjoy doing, and keep in mind that the ultimate reason any person exists is to bring glory to God. When you reflect on the third question, seriously ask yourself what God created you to do.

Dr. Falwell shares with us today that his *life plan* was developed by obeying what he knew he should do in each moment. The Lord gave him what he needed, when he needed it. What about you? What is your *life plan*, and how are you executing your plan to bring the maximum glory to God? Take into consideration the three questions above, and try to answer them in today's journal entry. Remember the important thing is to get moving and to keep moving forward for God.

Your Faith Journal Entry

Day Ten

INTENTIONAL PRAYER

Scripture Reading: Luke 11:1–13

Verse: "Ask, and it will be given to you; seek, and you will find; knock, and it will be opened to you." (Matthew 7:7)

Meditation:

Let me ask you a simple and silly question. When someone knocks on your door, what do you do? Hopefully you didn't say, "I hide in the back room!" When someone knocks on our doors, the usual response is to open the door and engage and help the person as much as we can. It's no different with our heavenly Father. He stands ready not only to hear our requests, but to aid and assist in the answer of our requests that are in keeping with His will.

In today's reading, Dr. Falwell gives us two important tips for developing an intentional prayer life. The first is to create a long prayer list of family and friends. As you pray daily through your list, you will think of additional names to add. Second, create a short prayer list of current problems and projects. Note any answers or partial answers as God responds to your requests.

In your journal today, begin creating your prayer lists and start specifically asking, seeking, and knocking. Remember that your heavenly Father stands ready to provide assistance, and He will open the door of heaven if you will just knock.

Your Faith Journal Entry

Day Eleven

GROWING THROUGH STEPS OF FAITH

Scripture Reading: Acts 16:6–40

Verse: "Since you excel in so many ways, grow in faith." (2 Corinthians 8:7, Falwell's translation)

Meditation:

Have you ever watched babies take their first steps? They have their hands all stretched out, and with a nervous look on their faces they boldly take a step or two, usually into the arms of a proud mother or father. Our spiritual development and walk with God is similar to our physical development. Just like a baby first learns to crawl, then to walk, and at last to run, we also should learn to "grow in our faith."

Perhaps the greatest legacy that Dr. Jerry Falwell will leave this world is his ability to believe God and to walk by faith. From building a church, to building a Christian K-12 school, to building a university and seminary, to influencing the political process, Dr. Falwell has learned to walk by faith. In today's reading, Dr. Falwell says, "When God puts a desire in you to do a task for Him, two things will happen. First, God will help you do it. Second, you'll grow your faith to trust Him for bigger things in the future."

In today's journal entry, reflect on some of your first steps of faith for God. What were they? How did you feel? What were the results? Also today, reflect on some possible next steps of faith you believe God may be asking you to take.

Your Faith Journal Entry

Day Twelve

FOCUSED PRAYER

Scripture Reading: Matthew 14:22–33

Verse: "Therefore do not be unwise, but understand what the will of the Lord is." (Ephesians 5:17)

Meditation:

What is the will of God for your life? The Bible tells us in Romans 12:1–2, "I beseech you therefore, brethren, by the mercies of God, that you present your bodies a living sacrifice, holy, acceptable to God, which is your reasonable service. And do not be conformed to this world, but be transformed by the renewing of your mind, that you may prove what is that good and acceptable and perfect will of God." This verse tells us plainly that if we take the time to read the Word of God and allow it to transform our minds, then we will "prove" or accomplish the good, acceptable, and perfect will of God. For most of us, discovering and doing the will of God is simply a matter of reading and obeying the Word of God.

In today's reading, Dr. Falwell says, "After you've yielded your present life to God's plan, then start searching for God's will in this matter by asking Him to show you what to do." Sometimes you must pray about something for a long time. Spending a long time in prayer "builds up your determination to see the issues brought to completion." In your journal, make a note of something you have been praying about for a long time. Also see if you can claim a scriptural promise or principle for the request, and begin praying a "focused prayer."

Your Faith Journal Entry

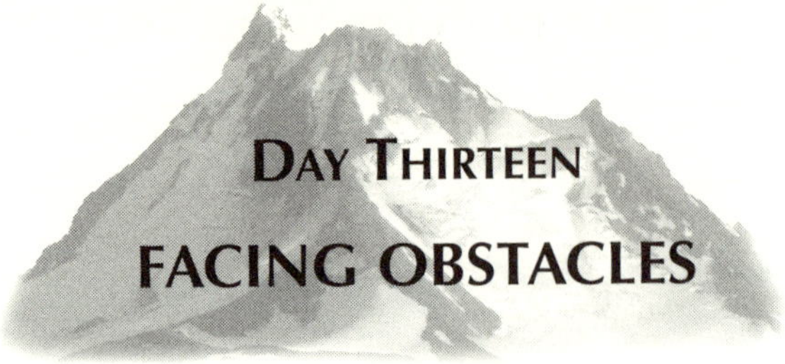

Day Thirteen

FACING OBSTACLES

Scripture Reading: Acts 11:19–30

Verse: "When it was clear, that he [Paul] wouldn't be dissuaded, we gave up and said, 'The will of the Lord be done.'" (Acts 21:14 TLB)

Meditation:

Newton's Third Law of Motion states, "For every action there is an opposite and equal reaction." This means that if something is moving forward, there is something else pushing it in the opposite direction. If you are a Christian, then you have several forces pulling you downward. First John 2:15–17 says that the world, the flesh, and the devil are all pulling the Christian in a downward direction. These downward forces are used to deceive, discourage, and dissuade us from accomplishing God's will. In addition, the Bible tells us, "Beloved, do not think it strange concerning the fiery trial which is to try you, as though some strange thing happened to you" (1 Pe 4:12).

This verse makes it clear we are going to face opposition. Sometimes the opposition we face in life may come from sources and people we never may have imagined.

In today's reading, the opposition to Dr. Falwell came from authority figures in his life, and that made it all the more difficult. Dr. Falwell reminds us, "When dealing with opposition, remember you belong to God alone and not to anything else on this earth." He also says to make sure you are right, and "make a decision then make it work." In your journal today, recount a time or two when you faced opposition and how you dealt with it.

Your Faith Journal Entry

DAY FOURTEEN
WALKING UNCHARTED PATHS

Scripture Reading: Acts 5:17–42

Verse: "By faith Abraham obeyed when he was called to go out to the place which he would receive as an inheritance. And he went out, not knowing where he was going." (Hebrews 11:8)

Meditation:

If you are like most people, you have at least one road map in your car, to help you determine how to get from point A to point B. Without the map, it would be difficult, if not impossible, for you to go to someplace new and different. With a clear map, however, you can chart a new course and direction. You can find a way out of your old place and routine. Of course, the road map for the Christian is the Word of God. We must go to the Word daily and find the directions we need.

On Day 14, Dr. Falwell gives us this advice: When you look at uncharted waters, "your first question should be, 'Is God in it?' Faith is doing what God tells you. Obviously, money, location, help, and equipment are all factors. But they're not the deciding factors. If God is in it . . . if people will be helped . . . if it fits scriptural boundaries . . . if you've prayed . . . then move ahead!"

In the verse above, Abraham didn't know where he was going, but he knew who was going with him. Sometimes that's all we have to go on, but it is more than enough. For today's journal entry, explore the faith steps you will need to fulfill your *life purpose.*

Your Faith Journal Entry

Day Fifteen

HOW CAN I HAVE MORE FAITH?

Scripture Reading: John 6:61–71

Verse: "As newborn babes, desire the pure milk of the word, that you may grow thereby." (1 Peter 2:2)

Meditation:

In Charles Dickens' classic *Oliver Twist,* poor Oliver asks for more gruel in this manner: "Please sir, I want some more." All of the adults were shocked because no one had ever asked for more. The Bible has a similar story when the poor widow goes to the unjust judge to ask for justice. The judge is at first unwilling, but because of the persistence of the widow he finally gives her what she wants. In the context of the story in Luke 18:1–8, Jesus says that our heavenly Father is not like the reluctant judge, but that He would answer our request "speedily." As Christians, we don't have to go to an unjust, impersonal judge; we can go to a loving and concerned Father who is interested in all of the details of our lives. He is so concerned about us that He has counted the number of the hairs on our head (Ma 10:30).

Dr. Falwell reminds us in today's reading to begin studying the Bible in a big way and to learn everything we can about the bigness of God. Apply what you learn from the Bible. "The bigger the things you attempt for God, the bigger your faith can grow." In your journal entry for today, list the biggest thing you believe God wants to do through you. Then move forward with Him to accomplish it.

Your Faith Journal Entry

Day Sixteen

GRASPING GOD'S WORD

Scripture Reading: Psalm 119:1–16

Verse: "But shun profane and vain babblings: for they will increase unto more ungodliness." (2 Timothy 2:16 KJV)

Meditation:

One thing that separates human beings from almost every species in God's creation is that we possess opposable thumbs. This means that we can grasp objects and hold on tightly when we need to. For example, when you pick up a book, you grasp with all four of your fingers, and your thumb closes the grasp so that you can pick up the book.

Many years ago the Navigators developed an illustration that showed how to get a good handle on the Word of God. You can get a good grasp on the Word if you use five habits. The first habit is to listen to the Scriptures through the preaching of the Word. The second is to read the Word, and the third is to study the Scriptures. Fourth, you can memorize the Word, and the fifth is the by-product of memorization, which is meditation. If you practice these five habits, you will have a tight grasp on the Word of God.

If you want to build dynamic faith, you must study and apply the Word of God. Take some time in your journal today and reflect on which of the five habits you need to strengthen.

Your Faith Journal Entry

Day Seventeen

CONVERSION IS JUST THE BEGINNING

Scripture Reading: John 3

Verse: "Therefore, if anyone is in Christ, he is a new creation; old things have passed away; behold, all things have become new." (2 Corinthians 5:17)

Meditation:

When we receive Christ, He comes into our lives and begins to make changes. Sometimes those changes are immediate. Others take several weeks or months. Sometimes we even wrestle with certain areas for the rest of our lives. Nevertheless, true conversion is the beginning of the end for the old nature. Second Corinthians 3:18 says, "But we all, with unveiled face, beholding as in a mirror the glory of the Lord, are being transformed into the same image from glory to glory, just as by the Spirit of the Lord." This transformation begins at conversion and is completed when we are translated into glory. We can definitely aid and assist this transformation process as we submit to God, resist the devil, and deal with sin daily.

Dr. Falwell, in this day's reading, gives us six statements to help us do a "spiritual checkup." In your journal today, note which of these you need to work on: One, "I have new spiritual desires to know God." Two, "I have new desires to learn the Scriptures." Three, "I have new desires to talk to God in prayer." Four, "I have a new burden to see my friends know God." Five, "I have a new desire to worship with Christians." Six, "I have a new desire to overcome sin and old habits."

Your Faith Journal Entry

Day Eighteen

DISCERNING FAITH

Scripture Reading: John 7:32–39

Verse: "Be filled with the Spirit" (Ephesians 5:18)

Meditation:

Discernment is defined as the "act or process of exhibiting keen insight and good judgment." How about you? Do you have discernment? This is so important because in order to build dynamic faith you also must build discernment to know what to do, how to do it, and when to practice the right habits.

In today's reading, Dr. Falwell tells the story of how a family in his church helped him to slow down and reflect on the nature and character of God. Mr. Whittemore's advice was this: "God doesn't want you to achieve great things in His name. He just wants you to love Him, to trust Him, to wait upon Him, and to praise Him. Then He can achieve what He desires through you." Dr. Falwell was working night and day building a new church. He was "working," but he was not allowing enough time for "waiting" on the Lord. It took discernment to recognize the "balance between my urge to win the world single-handedly and my deep desire to grow spiritually." An old statement sums this balance up nicely: "If you take care of the depth of your ministry, God will take care of the breadth of your ministry." What aspect do you need to work on, working or waiting?

Your Faith Journal Entry

Day Nineteen

MAKING FAITH STATEMENTS

Scripture Reading: Mark 11:12–26

Verse: "Jesus told His disciples: 'Have faith in God! If you have faith in God and don't doubt, you can tell this mountain to get up and jump into the sea, and it will.'" (Mark 11:22–23, Falwell's translation)

Meditation:

There is a fine line between being confident and being cocky. Confidence exhibits itself in a quiet assurance and is founded on inside information or knowledge that things will work out. Cockiness is a loud expression that is not founded on any evidence. Sometimes when we turn on the TV or radio we hear preachers telling us that they are sure that God will heal or deliver us from a situation or problem in which we find ourselves. They have faith in God's ability, but they don't necessarily have any "inside" information that God is also willing to assist us in the thing we desire from Him.

Today, Dr. Falwell explains the difference between making faith statements founded in the will of God and faith statements that originate from human desires. The main principle is found in 1 John 5:14–15 (Falwell's translation), "This is the confidence . . . that if we ask anything according to His will He hears us, and we know when He hears us, we have the answers we seek of Him." According to this verse, we must pray and fast and search the Scriptures until we hear clearly from the Lord. Once we hear clearly from the Lord, then we can announce to those around us, by faith, what we believe the Lord is going to do. That is making a "faith statement" that is pleasing to the Lord. Write in your journal today what mountain you believe God is getting ready to move in your life.

Your Faith Journal Entry

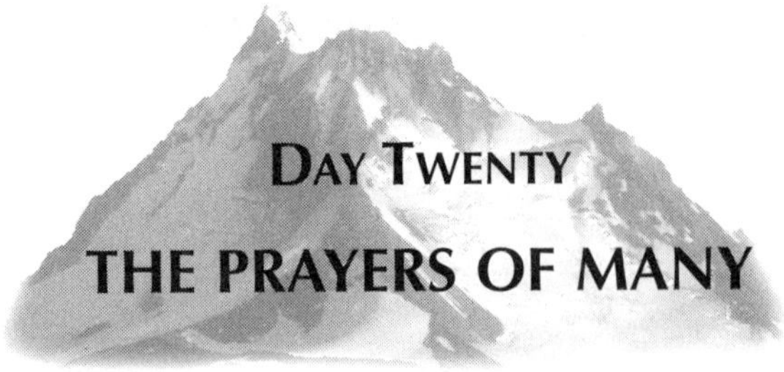

Day Twenty

THE PRAYERS OF MANY

Scripture Reading: Matthew 17:14–21

Verses: "And when they had prayed, the place where they were assembled together was shaken." (Acts 4:31)

"If two of you agree on earth concerning anything that they ask, it will be done for them by My Father in heaven." (Matthew 18:19)

Meditation:

Have you ever been involved in a tug-of-war? It's a simple game with simple rules. One rope. Two teams. The team that pulls the other over the line wins! Sometimes prayer feels this way, and it actually does work a bit like this. E. M. Bounds first made this statement that has been repeated often for the last 100 years: "Much prayer, much power; little prayer, little power; no prayer, no power." What this statement means is that sometimes in prayer we need "much prayer" or many people praying. Matthew 18:19 puts it this way: "If two of you agree on earth concerning anything that they ask, it will be done for them."

In today's reading, Dr. Falwell tells the story of how Vernon Brewer was delivered from cancer by the "prayers of many." More than five thousand students were praying for Vernon's healing, and the Lord heard their prayers. Dr. Falwell also gave a simple formula in today's reading: "The greater your obstacle or prayer request . . . the more people are needed to pray, the more often they must pray, the longer they must pray, and the more intensely they must pray."

In your journal entry today, list the biggest answer to prayer you have ever seen. Also take some time to list two or three people you could turn to if you needed some additional prayer partners.

Day Twenty-One

EXTREME CONDITIONS

Scripture Reading: Matthew 6:16–18; Ezra 8:21–36

se: "But when you fast . . . your Father, who sees in secret will ard you openly." (Matthew 6:16,18)

ditation:

at is the longest period of time you have gone without food? A ? A week? A month? A few hours? The dictionary defines *fast*-his way: "The act or practice of abstaining from or eating very food. A period of abstention or self-denial." The Scripture is when it says, "when you fast." Stated this way, it implies that ng will be a natural part of every Christian's life. Jesus put it g these lines, "Can the friends of the bridegroom mourn as as the bridegroom is with them? But the days will come when ridegroom will be taken away from them, and then they will ' Again fasting is expected from the followers of Jesus Christ, cially after the bridegroom (Jesus) has been taken away (after esurrection).

today's reading, Dr. Falwell shared the crisis that prompted o undertake two 40-day fasts. He was in an extreme condition new that a drastic situation called for drastic measures. Lib-University was on the verge of disaster and only God could it. Dr. Falwell knew that prayer and fasting is God's method sperate circumstances. Don't forget that fasting will not only se your body, it also will purify your motives. What moun-r crisis are you facing? Note in your journal today what tains need moving in your life.

Your Faith Journal Entry

Your Faith Journal Entry

Day Twenty-Two

HAVING CONTINUOUS REVIVAL

Scripture Reading: Psalm 139

Verse: "O LORD, You have searched me and known me." (Psalm 139:1)

Meditation:

Revival comes from two words, *vivere* meaning life and *re* meaning to do or to experience something again. So *revival* means "a restoration to use, acceptance, activity, or vigor after a period of obscurity." Many times in our spiritual life we go through periods where God seems distant or far away. Usually this distance is because of our selfish decisions that lead to sin. When we move far away from God, He chooses not to use us, and as a result we are not far away from obscurity. In today's reading, we discover principles related to experiencing continuous revival, or how to draw near to God and stay near to Him.

Dr. Falwell comments on this subject. "Two steps are necessary to lead you to revival. First, let God show you your sinfulness in light of His holiness. Second, make sure your hands are clean before God. When you have clean hands and a pure heart, then you will be able to pray with power. Then you should get results from your prayers." First John 1:9 says, "If we confess our sins, He is faithful and just to forgive us our sins and to cleanse us from all unrighteousness." In your journal today record and confess a couple of areas where the old nature has been getting the best of you lately.

Your Faith Journal Entry

Day Twenty-Three

THINKING THE UNTHINKABLE

Scripture Reading: Philippians 4:1–20

Verse: "Now to Him who is able to do exceedingly abundantly above all that we ask or think, according to the power that works in us." (Ephesians 3:20)

Meditation:

In the above verse the apostle Paul challenges the Ephesian church that God can do "exceedingly and abundantly above all that we ask or think." It's like God in heaven is just waiting for someone to ask for something so big and so challenging that when someone finally does ask Him for that thing He wants to do and that only He can do, God graciously complies.

In today's reading, Dr. Falwell relays the events of the summer of 2004 and says, "Everything on Liberty Mountain came together: an abundance of new buildings, paved roads, sports facilities, and much more. . . . Without a doubt, in 2004 we saw more answers to prayer, moved to have more students educated, and spent more money in a single period of time than ever—more than $23 million—and we didn't have to borrow. God supplied in a magnificent way."

You may not need to raise $23 million, but whether you need $23 million or $10. . . if you don't have it and need it . . . the provision is still a miracle. God will supply and meet the need in His timing. In your journal today, don't forget that God "wants to do exceedingly and abundantly beyond all that we could ask or think." Don't let human limitation affect your thinking. Take a few minutes to dream some big dreams!

Your Faith Journal Entry

Day Twenty-Four

SYMPATHY IN ACTION

Scripture Reading: Galatians 5:16–25

Verse: "And on some have compassion, making a difference." (Jude 22 KJV)

Meditation:

In the Gospel of Matthew, the Scripture records for us that when Jesus looked out upon the multitudes, He felt "compassion" for them. The compassion that Jesus experienced always moved Him to action. He didn't just see the need and have sympathetic feelings. He responded and met the need. In the Book of James, seeing a need and not acting is condemned: "If a brother or sister is naked and destitute of daily food, and one of you says to them, 'Depart in peace, be warmed and filled,' but you do not give them the things which are needed for the body, what does it profit?" (2:15–16). This is a rhetorical question because the answer is that it profits nothing.

Throughout Dr. Falwell's life and ministry, feeling compassion and acting have gone together. In today's reading, Dr. Falwell recounts the humble beginnings of "Elim Home for Alcoholics." The ministry started with just two men seeking deliverance from the destructive and highly addictive drug. Building dynamic faith is not simply a matter of "walking on water" just for the sake of doing the impossible. Building dynamic faith means that we are acting in concert and cooperation with God's Spirit to meet the needs of those people for whom the Son of God died.

In your journal, jot down the names of two or three people to whom you could show compassion, and also note specifically some things you could do to put words into action.

Your Faith Journal Entry

Day Twenty-Five

LEARNING FROM MISTAKES

Scripture Reading: 2 Corinthians 1:3–11

Verse: "All these, having obtained a good testimony through faith, did not receive the promise." (Hebrews 11:39)

Meditation:

This may be difficult, or even painful, to answer, but what is the worst mistake you have ever made? It could be a financial mistake, or a relational mistake, or a spiritual mistake, or it could be a combination of several areas. Part of the reason for keeping a journal is to reflect on your life—where you have been, where you are currently, and where you are going. There is great value to take the time to reflect on our mistakes, because if we don't learn from the mistakes of our past, we are bound to make the same mistakes in the future.

Dr. Falwell relates that in 1973 his greatest mistake was not having his "financial house" in order. As a result, the church faced the possibility of being shut down by the Securities and Exchange Commission. This was a serious mistake, and it had very real and serious consequences. In this dark hour, Jerry learned several important lessons. First, set your eyes on God and not on your problems. Second, talk to God continually. Third, have many people praying for you. Fourth, never be afraid to examine what you're doing, and, fifth, wait for God's release that comes after you admit your mistakes.

Go ahead, pull back the bandage and look at the scar of your big mistake. Confess it to God and seek His forgiveness.

Your Faith Journal Entry

Day Twenty-Six

WINNING AGAIN AFTER A BIG LOSS

Scripture Reading: Job 1–2

Verse: "'Naked I came from my mother's womb, and naked shall I return there. The Lord gave, and the Lord has taken away; blessed be the name of the Lord.' In all this Job did not sin, nor charge God with wrong." (Job 1:21–22)

Meditation:

One reason most people enjoy sports is because of the drama of athletic competition. There are winners and there are losers. We enjoy watching how the winners react, and we also learn lessons from the person or team on the "short end of the stick." In many ways, life is a lot like sports. Sometimes we stand, exhausted, after a great victory and enjoy the euphoric rush of a hard-fought win. Many more times, however, we pick ourselves up off the mat after getting knocked out by an uppercut we didn't see coming.

In today's reading, Dr. Falwell talks about the many times in his life and ministry when he wondered if he would make it to the next day. In the reading, we learn of another man, Job, who probably also wondered if he would make it to the next day. In one day, Job lost his wealth and possessions, his health, and his children. The Bible records for us "that in all this Job did not sin, nor charge God with wrong." In your journal today, reflect on the times when you had the wind knocked out of you. How did you react? How did God see you through the loss? What lessons did you learn?

Your Faith Journal Entry

Day Twenty-Seven

REJOICING IN VICTORY

Scripture Reading: Acts 18:1–11; Nehemiah 4; 6:15–16

Verse: "So the wall was finished . . . in fifty-two days. And [our enemies and the surrounding nations] perceived that this work was done by our God." (Nehemiah 6:15–16)

Meditation:

What has been the greatest spiritual victory you have ever seen or experienced? Perhaps God has delivered you from a past hurt, habit, or hang-up. Perhaps you have seen God "part the Red Sea" for you and destroy the pursuing cloud of darkness. Perhaps the Lord has avenged you from someone who was trying to hurt you. Whatever the case may be, how do you respond when you see the hand of God deliver you from the enemy and set your feet on solid ground? Hopefully you can be humble enough to recognize, like the children of Israel did in the verse above, and perceive "that this work was done by our God" and appropriately give Him the credit for the victory.

Building dynamic faith means that we will regularly see God moving mountains and casting them into the sea! When this occurs, we also must be careful to show our appreciation to our great and gracious God. In today's reading, Dr. Falwell gives some pointers for rejoicing in victory: First, create a list of praises. Second, put an asterisk next to obvious victories and, third, purposefully praise God for your victories and what they mean to you. In your journal today list 10 things you are thankful for and praise God for providing them.

Your Faith Journal Entry

Day Twenty-Eight

LEARNING FAITH IN DEFEAT

Scripture Reading: James 1:1–18

Verse: " . . . knowing that the testing of your faith produces patience." (James 1:3)

Meditation:

The dictionary defines *defeat* as "A failure to win. A coming to naught; frustration: e.g. *the defeat of a lifelong dream.*" What is an ongoing frustration in your life? Today's reading is about learning to deal with situations in our lives that we fail to win and the subsequent frustration that comes with the defeat.

An ongoing frustration for Dr. Falwell and millions of other Christians began on January 23, 1973, when the Supreme Court overruled "state laws that prohibit voluntary abortions before the third month." This one ruling has kept millions of unborn babies from seeing the light of day. Dr. Falwell says this about abortion: "I think I've done everything spiritually, politically, and physically I could do to reverse the tide of abortion in America. We win a few battles against abortion, then we lose some other battle. It's not over and I'm not giving up."

What battles have you been fighting in which you haven't seen a positive answer or victory? Here are some principles from Dr. Falwell that may help you keep going: First, you are winning the inner battle just because you've entered the fray. Second, keep fighting when you're right, not just when you're successful. Third, know that we may not win on this earth, but there is a greater victory in heaven. Fourth, keep your eyes on Jesus. In your journal today, write about the areas on which you need to concentrate.

Your Faith Journal Entry

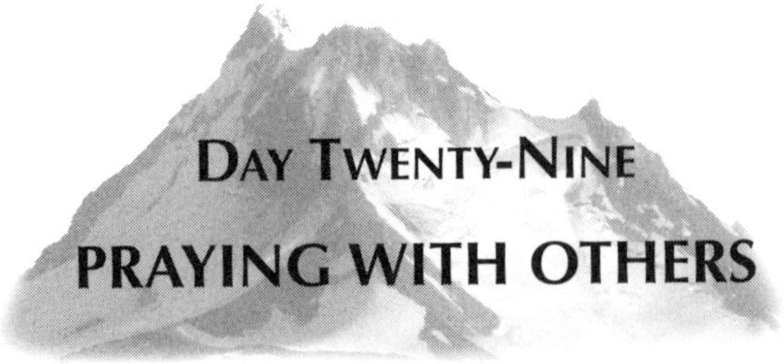

Day Twenty-Nine

PRAYING WITH OTHERS

Scripture Reading: Exodus 17:5–16

Verse: "Again I say to you that if two of you agree on earth concerning anything that they ask, it will be done for them by My Father in heaven." (Matthew 18:19)

Meditation:

Ecclesiastes 4:9–12 says, "Two are better than one, because they have a good reward for their labor. For if they fall, one will lift up his companion. But woe to him who is alone when he falls, for he has no one to help him up. Again, if two lie down together, they will keep warm; but how can one be warm alone? Though one may be overpowered by another, two can withstand him. And a threefold cord is not quickly broken."

The principle of two being better than one is taught throughout the Bible. Part of being human is that, periodically, we need encouragement to keep going. Mark Twain said, "I can live up to two months on a good compliment." Woe to the person who has no one to help him when he falls down. Not only do we need people to help us when we fall, but we also need help when we face opposition. Dr. Falwell, in today's reading, makes this statement: "Without prayer partners, I'm convinced there wouldn't be a Liberty University, nor would Thomas Road Baptist Church have the great influence it has. What God has done for me, He has done with the help of many others."

In your journal today, make a list of people for whom you are praying, and also make a list of people who are praying for you.

Your Faith Journal Entry

Day Thirty

WHEN YOUR FAITH DOESN'T SEEM TO WORK

Scripture Reading: Daniel 3

Verse: "O Nebuchadnezzar . . . our God whom we serve is able to deliver us from the burning fiery furnace, and He will deliver us from your hand, O king. But if not, let it be known to you, O king, that we do not serve your gods, nor will we worship the gold image which you have set up." (Daniel 3:16–18)

Meditation:

What is the best idea you have ever had? Sometimes our ideas are well received, and sometimes they just don't seem to get off the ground. In today's reading, Dr. Falwell tells about his idea of having 100,000 home classes across America, composed of Faith Partners, gathering their friends together to study the Bible. He also shares the "rest of the story" that no matter what he tried, he was never able to get the idea moving in the right direction.

How can we determine when God is leading us and the other times when we are leading ourselves? Again we have some principles from today's reading: First, review your answers to prayer. Look back over the last 30 days and check those items where you know God heard and answered. Second, take the time to honestly reflect. Reflection gives you the ability to gain insights from events to discern how God works. Third, practice honest confession. When you've got it wrong, admit it. There is no sense in quibbling when your idea is not from God. The sooner you realize it, the better. Fourth, thank God for the non-answers, because those are answers too. Remember God answers prayers in this manner: Yes, no, or wait.

Reflect in your journal today one idea of yours that was evidently not from God. What did you learn from it?

Your Faith Journal Entry

Day Thirty-One

TODAY COUNTS

Scripture Reading: Hebrews 11:1–12:2

Verse: "Therefore we also, since we are surrounded by so great a cloud of witnesses, let us lay aside every weight, and the sin which so easily ensnares us, and let us run with endurance the race that is set before us, looking unto Jesus, the author and finisher of our faith." (Hebrews 12:1–2)

Meditation:

Have you ever tried to run with weights on your ankles or wrists? If you have, you know how liberating it is when those weights are taken off. Your legs feel much lighter when you are released from the weights. This study has been designed to help you "run with patience the race that is set before you." We have spent the last month talking about building dynamic faith. Let's end this month of study by focusing on Jesus. He is the "finisher of our faith." That means you live each day by faith in Him because He is your God.

It is important to build your life on a firm foundation, and there is no firmer foundation than the Lord Jesus Christ. In your journal, on this last day, again write out your *life purpose*. Also look back over the past 30 days and record the most significant discovery from your journal entries. It could be a principle from the Word or an insight from God's Spirit. Perhaps it is a lesson you learned a long time ago, or it could be a lesson you have just recently mastered. Whatever the case, in order to build dynamic faith, we must keep our eyes on Jesus because He is "the author and finisher of our faith!"

Your Faith Journal Entry